Without a dog

Julia Deakin

graft
poetry

2008

Published 2008
Graft Poetry
34 Peckover Street
Bradford BD1 5BD
West Yorkshire

Printed by Inprint + Design, Bradford
Cover design: www.cloudspotting.co.uk

ISBN 978-0-9558400-0-5

A CIP catalogue record for this book is available from the British Library

ACKNOWLEDGEMENTS

Thanks are due to the editors of the following, who first published some of these poems:
Acumen, Aireings, Anon, Envoi, Fighting Cock Press, Northern Exposure, nth Position, Orbis, Octavo, Pennine Platform, Poetry Monthly, Raw Edge, Stand, Staple, The North and *The Rialto*. 'Twentieth century' was a runner-up in the Wells Competition 2002. 'War poem' won third prize in the Shrewsbury Literary Festival 2003, and 'Unattributed sampler' won first prize in the *Northern Exposure* Poetry Competition 2006.

CONTENTS

About slithering

Misadventure

Escapology

Learning to kiss

Without a dog

About slithering

About slithering
Sue Ryder Christmas Card

Here they come now beetling across the mantelpiece
on skates like harpoons under heavy skirts or sagging ochre leggings
heading out to party party at the flat world's edge.

One couple's overdressed for this, she in her apron frills and ruff,
he in puff pantaloons, some kind of hothead weapon at the hip;
behind, three cloak-and-dagger types in cavalier hats poke fun
while bottom right two lads who have just vandalised a privy
to expose a backside in full flow run off, half scandalised themselves.
Even the fenceposts totter drunkenly as if inclined to start something.

What is this glassy limboland though? Where does earth end
and the sky begin? Beyond the painter's unseen high ground
and some sketchy reed banks there is no relief
and from the shanty town of sheds and huts,
with every craft that might have floated hopelessly holed up,
a sinking feeling spreads.

Is it the trees' black fingers cracking up the sky?
The hellish props – tattered windbreaks, gibbets, joint stools –
fished from Hieronymus's skip? The dearth of decent carpenters?
Or just the sunlessness – the only warmth a puny blaze
lit recklessly in mid-ice?

Far right there's half a posher red-bricked house,
its odd hipped gable partly covering a dark high window
like a cowled eye.

Below, a woman at a stable door observes,
not softened by the winter's smile.

Unattributed sampler

Bankfield Regimental Museum, Halifax

IN MEMORY OF ELIZABETH HITCHEN, WHO DIED NOvember 26, this battle was begun in 1841. The house was quiet *and you must learn to be,* Grandmamma whispered, measuring the lines. *Your little sister's gone* AGED 13 MONTHS *to be with God.*

I was just five but could already read THEY WILL BE MISST A VACANT PLACE AT TABLE AND AT TIME OF PRAYER. *What shall we put up there* I asked, *in the big space? Lord knows, my love – God will decide she said,* then smiled. *Me, probably.*

AT HOME AT CHURCH MORN NOON AND NIGHT she printed carefully MISST ALL THE TIME AND EVERY WHERE. With the next letter, G – she stopped. *When you're a big girl, you can do the rest.* Next day she showed me cross-stitch and I sewed IN MEMORY until my eyes hurt.

Eight years slipped by AND ALSO ASSENETH WHO DIED when I was thirteen FEB 8 1849. That night I satin-stitched an urn, an altar, half a rose. AGED 19 MONTHS. The cloth was grey by then with childish sweat, pinpricks of blood and also tears AND ALSO

HANNAH two years on THE GRANDMOTHER OF THE ABOVE. I found the last lines of the verse she had left off and marked them up, but couldn't frame – until I'd lived as long again – to add 'on' to the G ON BUT NOT LOST OH THIS WE KNOW

– my nephew feverish, I had to end this tale. Thread by thread I drew our family back AND ALSO EMILY my niece WHO DIED AGED 4 YEARS AND 4 MONTHS AND ALSO JOHN their father WHO DIED 1865 AGED 28 AND ALSO AZUBAH WHO DIED AGED 18 YEARS and all so young.

WE KNOW WE TRUST I persevered THE BOUNDLESS LOVE stitching my fingers numb OF GOD HE DOETH ill John's son was ill, fighting for breath aged 4. If I could break the spell I told myself and stitch one living name – my own – with some date soon perhaps all would be WELL

HIS WILL BE DONE WE SAY AND KISS his eyes his hands his fingernails *God will decide* my needle vain to stop HIS CHASTENING ROD claiming one more AND ALSO for this field of crosses

MICHAEL HITCHEN WHO DIED JUNE 5 1872 AGED 4 the 'years' elided AND 10 MONTHS.

When I was six
Lotus shoes, early 1900s, The Tolson Museum

they broke my ankles and bound my feet.
They said it wouldn't hurt when they put me to sleep
but when I woke it did and when I tried to stand
I fell and gashed my face and lay and screamed
and a nurse and my maid Suyin came running
and said *don't cry, with your tiny feet
you'll be the envy of Szechuan.*
                      Dressing my face,
nurse said I'd be lucky not to have a scar –
but when they unwound the bandages and saw
my feet, blue-black as a typhoon, the shape and smell
of rotting vegetables, I said *do you want that then,
is that what you want* and they looked away,
busying themselves as I lay, listening to their feet.

You will be beautiful my father said, as if
it were an order and I said *was I not that already
had I not been a perfect baby then* and he said
you know that isn't what I mean and me
this is the twentieth century not the tenth and him
the more you argue the more you prove my case.
What case, I said, *what case?*
                      I looked at mother
who was silent. Later she said why didn't I paint
or practise holding my fan, looking ladylike…
that I should be grateful for a life of ease,
only having to bow and look serene.
But she did not look at me then, or when, married
at fifteen, I told her the day they broke my feet
still seemed like yesterday.

You're lucky, says Suyin, brazen now,
you can sit around all day and think
how beautiful you'll be — you are... as she walks
away. You *are not meant to walk but glide*
they say, but I can only shuffle. My husband grunts
he married a lady not a labourer and anyway
he likes me better lying down.

                     Opium helps,
but sometimes I wake myself screaming
you said it wouldn't hurt when you put me to sleep
and to my father, truly deaf now, *what case, what case*
and to my mother *ladylike* and to my husband
off somewhere and Suyin, in her own oblivion.
Tears run into my ears, along a faint scar.

It's not what we sent you to college for

I called you Laurence Stephen – a plain enough name
I thought, but dignified – and prayed
that some day you'd be an artist
like Dante Gabriel Rossetti.

Dante Gabriel Rossetti, now there was a name
to conjure with – and yes, he conjured goddesses.
Full-throated creatures, larger than life,
who filled the canvas with a sigh
that left you breathless –

but what have you done? What do you paint
larger than life? 'A mass of humanity'? A mess.
Your figures hump-backed, scurrying, bent double…
daren't they stand up straight, your men?
Layabouts, dogs and grim hags
at people's backs, like death.

I paint what I see, mother.

All these years I've waited for
a sign, one line of artistry –
and what have you given me? Smudges.
Spoil heaps. Rivers like cesspools.
Shiftless crowds. The eye directionless.
Not making sense of the world –

– then maybe it doesn't make sense –

– you could have done so well. You used to draw
but now you daub. You could have made your name,
like Dante Gabriel Rossetti – poetic and angelic –
now he could paint. Your landscapes sprawl.

You speak for yourself, mother.
I speak for millions, son.

And cripples! What do you paint them for?
Sometimes I don't know where to look.

Then why don't you look at me, mother?
Why don't you look at me?

Praha

Prague.
A palace on every corner
but in the Jewish quarter
a multi-storey cemetery,

a century of graves
on top of one another –
five, six, seven generations
in as many feet
scrambling petrified
in death towards the light.

Turning, you feel
their breath
and hear the rasp
of an old, ill-fitting
door.

Praha (Czech) *n. doorstep. Legend says the city stands where the head of its founding dynasty saw a man building a doorstep.*

Pueblo blanco

You have lugged your summer-hunger here,
unpacked and put away reminders of the long haul,
tortuous, through landscapes desiccated
under gas-flame skies, bends slung like shelving
over parched ravines,

bone-coloured hardcore scarring bluffs and screes,
the stuff of ambushes – *the horses tense, uneasy…*
then three silhouettes against the ridge, a minor key –
to scan yet one more wilderness of rocks
where surely nobody can live, so far
from everything?

Round one last corner, pitched like old fridges
up a hill you have caught sight of 'your' village;
nearer, thought the shed emitting screams
must be the school at first but later found out
was the slaughterhouse

making *chorizos,* for which piglets squeal
into the small hours – white noise you almost shut out,
like the doorstep fracas and the dawn loudhailer
calling initiates to trainers, dusty videos,
strange underwear.

Then you have stepped out, midday mad dogs
hunting food, a baker's – drawing blanks, uncertain
even of the way to walk discreetly down
these cobbled slopes, sandals slapping loudly, pinkness
putting pot plants in the shade;

peered surreptitiously at window stickers, crept
like thieves, half-hearing *Bread!*
The hour for bread is gone. This is the hour for –

titters. TVs flickering from fly-screen doors
like women smiling in chador;

you've longed to shrink enough to shuffle
like the bent black figures, alleyway to alleyway;
felt your limbs gross as loaves, your wants
profligate: bread and a drink – something you recognise
and can pronounce;

while from the white heat you have glimpsed
the dark insides of bars, whose padded seat backs,
strip lit, pulsate, as behind you
through the whitewash, you become aware
of something hissing.

Checkpoint

We come from hell. A history of short measures, rough justice,
public executions. Rules of thumb. From backs bent in fields,
mines and furnaces, we walked miles in rags through becks
clogged with debris, hitching lifts on carts down rutted tracks
or shut for days in cramped, smoky carriages on splintered slats
with cocky strangers leering legally,
                                        to cities ruled by horses
in the hands of drunks, the sound of klaxons, screeching,
oaths and tolling bells obscuring backstreet screams of birth,
crude amputations, barber dentists, TB wheezing up the stairs,
spit and spittoons everywhere, cataracts and goitres rampant,
fingers green with nicotine and ink, the tang of coins fished
from gutters, rivers heaving with the dead. Rain and slime
between our toes came with us into dim rooms close with soot
and sulphur, clogging nostrils picked for smuts flicked into rugs
thick with grit, chairs with dust and hair oil, privies cold
and wet or fetid, just vacated, hands from here unwashed
to hack food with a penknife used for fingernails and hooves
in kitchens home to cats, dogs, beetles, maggots, grubs in fruit
and slugs in greens at tables wiped with cloths boiled with kerchiefs,
bandages and nappies brought from bedrooms shared with mice,
bedbugs, nitcombs, pisspots, plaster peeling onto damp bolsters,
clammy sheets and memories of leeches, layings-out and wakes,
clothes seamed with sweat heaped souring in moth-filled closets
next to pictures over mould and trapped birds in chimney breasts
and hard soap scum in aluminium tubs of cooling water
fanned by draughts from grey net at the streaming windows,
springtails in the rotten frames and in the attic, books and papers
pulverised, riddled rafters, wasps' nests, pigeon lime.

We're here now. Gated, lighted. Vaccinated, regulated.
Vacuumed, smokeless, enzyme clean. It's been
so long, like centuries.

Everything stank. Tanneries and pits and breath.
This is the past. Do not turn us back.

Misadventure

Two girls, aged nine and ten

It was the blue in all those blacks and browns –
the sudden smoothness in the cross-hatched twigs
as if the hedge had all along had four blue eyes:
ingots of sky, sent down for us alone – that held us.
This was it, then: proof of fairies, heaven,
aliens and Father Christmas
all in one.

Two or three we'd just look at, but four or five
and all the ingenuity, the nerve and brilliance
of an intrigue hatched behind our backs
almost, would make us touch that downy cup
to feel its pewter roundness and then take
one keepsake, just one,
from the dream.

And when in other places we found more
and no one stopped us when we asked for needles,
cotton wool and boxes, or we showed them off
to visitors who praised our neatness and enthused
about the miracle of life, it was a miracle
nobody seemed to think
it was a crime.

Misadventure

They put you to bed, to sleep, at dusk but
you stayed up late, hearing the voices downstairs.

They left you alone but you crept back down
behind them, step by step, crossing the frontier.

They made sure you were safe but you waded
through wave after wave, further and further

out of your depth toeing armchairs, drifts,
the rise and fall of how adults thought and talked,

teased by shivery fronds. What they could laugh at
without you. The undertow. The far horizons.

Small dreams of a doormat

I shall do such things... what they are yet I know not
        – King Lear

Go on then – don't make eye contact
just walk all over me, I know my place
among the lowest of the low, pushed into doorways
under everything and everyone;
you'd put me right out if you could, except – I have my uses.
Wipe yourself off on me then call me dirty? We shall see.
It's murder here: the wind whistles viciously under the draught excluder
and I bear the brunt of every booted stranger like a scar.

Smutty bastards, lady mucks! I harbour grime:
caked and hardened to a crust its dust becomes me
and my filthy mind. Biding my time, dreaming low-down dreams
of multicoloured silken-tufted flying carpets
morning and evening, from your going out until your coming in
night after night, year after year
I lie here, bristling.

Room

The room at the end of the hall
on the fifth floor at the back of the block
was mine. The coldest smallest room
in the dullest saddest apartment
in the city. The bed –

How can an apartment be sad
you ask. *Isn't that a lazy word*
for a poet? No, I use the word
advisedly. A pathetic fallacy perhaps
but not pathetic. The place reeked
of sadness. The floorboards creaked
sadly. The twigs in pots were sad.
My employers, Mr & Mrs Sadly
unsuited, their son, Sadly conceived,
and their dog, Sadly confined.

The taps leaked sadness.
You filled your cup with it.
The patch at the top of the landing
oozed it. The oven infused each dish
with it the carpet was stained with it
the ornaments sat in it the papers
covered it, the mirrors doubled it.
The view from every room
that had a view and mine didn't –
mine was of a brick wall
down a light well –

well, you get the picture. And
you woke up at dead of night
racked with sadness. Not just me
but everyone there at times
and in their own time. The place
was sad, sad, sad. And if that

makes this a bad poem maybe
poetry is the poorer, not to hear
sadness when it's spoken of,
not to make room for words
that exist because sometimes,
sadly, there is no other word.

There
i.m. Diane and Annika, drink-drive victims
killed as they walked home from celebrating their move into a new house.

Not in the empty house unlocked by next of kin at 5am,
the little nest of mugs and plates in water not yet cold…
not in the folded limbs of clean socks and t-shirts waiting to be put away,
the tins of paint, the brushes soaking in white spirit…
not in the two names ringing from the clutch of letters,
not in the prized quiet of their double bed…
not in the smiles from the sideboard
nor yet in the open daily paper on the sofa…
not in the distant sirens
or the cat clawing…

but afterwards
over and over,
under the twisted metal, the piles of settling dust, the shrouds of fabric,
under the scorching ashes sifted through with teaspoons,
through the acrid fumes in the arc-lit tunnel behind the bulkhead
downstream, under the rock, caught in branches
under the shale, the mud, the weight of snow
in the crush of timber in the pitch-black flooded chasm
under the rubble torn at with bare hands
there,
over and over
they will find their child.

Q.E.D.

That you can reconstruct a life from dust –
that each of us signs the air we breathe,
the clothes we wear, the articles we touch –

the pilgrim kissing a bone, the lover
saving a lock of hair, the orphan
folding a letter and the widower
opening a drawer
have always known.

Sleepless

Fixing your eyes dead centre on the road
you turn the radio down low and pull
your thoughts back from the verge of morbid dreams
to better times ahead. Even the sleet
now softening to snow seems kind – like life
relaxing. Yes! You'd get things right this time.

Four thirty, getting on for dawn. Best time
to use the motorways these days. The roads
deserted – not a sign of human life.
High on adrenaline – and her – you pull
your mind back to the job in hand. Sleet
swirling at you now, like those strange dreams

you move through saying *this is just a dream.*
Or last night on the phone. Where had the time
gone? When you're having fun it flies, like sleet
melts, instantly, into the past – the road
behind – and you fly too, till something pulls
you back – some sudden crisis stops your life

dead in its tracks... but then that's life's
rich pattern for you. In your worst dreams
or nightmares these things happen, but you pull
through – when the alarm goes, sometimes
at the very moment – *weird, that.* Bad road
and you're tired – talking to yourself. Sleet

falling. Falling. Walking. Waking. Sleet
across the tracks. Can't be. The tracks. Life
flashing past you like a train that's left the road
the line the phone call 999 bad dreams
get back! *Please, help – there might not be much time
and – there's a train coming!* Not waking, pull

your eyes back open. Sick. But must… and pull
yourself back to your feet and move through sleet
and darkness to the horror of the time
that from now on you'll have to call your life.
That scene, those screams will be your waking dreams
until your wished-for death blocks off the road.

Now you pull back your sleeve to inject dreams:
a sleet-cold, straight black vein your only road
back to another time, another life.

War poem

Today we have
an individual carton of fruit squash.
Arthritic fingers fumble
for the ridge – the clear cellophane
his failing eyes can't see –
which holds the straw diagonally
down one side.

Stiff joints scrabble for the loose edge
next and numbly strain to grasp it.
Fingers and thumbs, then, grip the sachet
and pull, with weak wrists – pull –
to rip it open. Fish out the straw,
feel for its point
and pause, exhausted.

Now, trembling, turn the pack
and squint to see the foil spot –
weak skin to be breached.
Hold firmly but don't squeeze the sides
and briskly push the straw in.
Again – it slips and bends. Again.
A little spills, dribbling down his blazer cuff.

He sighs, pushing the straw in further.
How much easier to bayonet the eyes.

Her voice

Eighteen months a widower
you, thinner than ever, step in from the hard November garden
to that light, airy room, the linen covers with the orange blossom
I remember her so proud of
faded, now, to almost white.

You brew tea, find *KitKats* got in by your married son or daughter
and soon talk readily about her pain, her faith, your lack of it,
life's cruelty and how you never would have guessed till now…
and how among the memories you stumble over every day
you try and try but still you can't recall her voice, her voice…

It will come back, I say, *in time*
(wondering why I can hear its shot silk timbre –
a smoker's, though she wasn't – loud and clear
as if she were sitting next to you, or me)
and then I hear someone – Steve in his nurse's voice, or me, or her –
saying *you must look after yourself*
and you, how you've never been interested in food
or seen what people see in it
and then, matter-of-factly, coming to your own trouble,
which we know something of (the too familiar chronicle
of oversights, referrals and delays),
raising your shirt to show us, half way up,
your own tumour, huge as a boxer's gloved fist, in your back.

And I hear nothing, rushing
like the sea in a shell to my ear
but her voice, her voice. Her voice.

Cuckoo

And always afterwards
the thought returns:
the time, the place, the light, the look
rewind and replay of their own accord.

The act undone, the words unsaid come back
and burn themselves into the retina,
scavenge scraps, smother memory
and sing and sing

one time, one place, one angle of the light
and always afterwards.

Escapology

Where I come from

was a smokeless zone, a village
without pavements.

Our house was a whitewashed bungalow –
the biggest sheet of paper you've ever seen –
which one day I decided to draw on.

I got a piece of coke and drew a house
with two storeys, the kind you read about
in stories about people who live in towns.

I added curtains to the windows, flowers
to the curtains, steps up to the front door
and a long coil of smoke, arcing
towards Stoke-on-Trent.

When Dad came round the corner
he went mad. Said it made the place
look like a slum.

I thought it was a good drawing.
A nicer house than ours.

J'accuse

When next door got a chubby Morris Minor –
a sage-green Billy Bunter of a car
with goggling headlamps, pimply side lights,
homely wooden trim and flapping indicators
signalling the urge to fly,

we got a raffish, low-slung Triumph Herald,
red and white, all pointy finials and chrome fingernails.
Rusting before the year was out, it dragged us
through our childhood, shedding its paint
and scabby chassis all round Warwickshire,
making my mother misread maps
and my father misread everything, while we sat
in the back on clammy coffee-coloured seats
that stank and stuck your bare legs to them,
fishing cornflakes out of shallow tupperware
and watching the windows cry.
Glimpsed from here,
the swinging sixties passed us by.

Gone

The things you gave me I still have:

I
the scraps of fabric and the six-inch piece
of gold-striped ribbon salvaged
from beneath your mum's machine;

the plastic roe deer which has stood
with its sellotaped hind leg
on every windowsill I've had;

a secret knowledge of *Bewitched*
and other stuff on ITV
we weren't supposed to watch at home;

and turns of phrase. *I'm used to it* the first
I gleaned from you at six, your hands in icy water
thawing pyramids of school milk.

(By nine those hands were battlefields I saw
as, sitting bare-kneed on the cloakroom steps
we pored over each other's scabs.)

II
And words. Like when you scratched your head
and showed me the results: *That's scurf, that is;*

and *Swarfega* – that was one of your best
(plus the tip that butter would do as well).

And the round blue toffee tin with the squirrel on
that's been in the tool box ten years
labelled *Longer screws;*

and awe. For you were surely
twice the family we were –
your sister, all but grown up
with her dyed black, back-combed hair,
your brother the stock car racer
and blue-eyed Julian, just five;

and pride. When I fell headlong
in your dung-filled milking shed
I watched your bleach-blonde mum
in her space-age kitchen *spin dry* all my clothes
which I carried, ironed and smelling of *Tide* not *Omo*
home like the World Cup in a paper bag;

and respect. You were the brightest
in our year, my Dad, the school head, said –
but yours wouldn't let you take the 11-plus.
Not worth it for a girl, he said;

and dreams of Craig, who being your cousin
(though half the school were that) meant
I'd never have to fight you for him;

and my first postcard from anywhere
addressed to me, from Aberystwyth
with only one spelling mistake.

(Your last family holiday, that turned out to be
before we left, your mum and dad 'parted'
and you, she and Julian moved out.)

III
And every Halloween (your birthday)
a sense of magic at the stars and dark;

and the snap you sent me, when you got engaged
of you and Vinnie in a Blackpool photo booth;

and an interest in your namesake Vivien Leigh
and half a mind to read *Gone with the Wind*
one day when I'm stuck somewhere;

and a taste for Spain –
though I've not been to Benidorm
where the last I heard you worked as a courier
and had gone to live for good

as far from childhood as you could.

Prescription

The wig sat at the bottom of the wardrobe
in a deep, square, dark blue box
like a hat or ashes or some strange stage prop.

They sent it out before you started chemo
so you wouldn't feel you couldn't face the world –
or if you stayed in wouldn't feel undressed, or cold.

You tried it, once. It sat on your thinned hair
like no hat any body ever wore or hair they grew
but thicker, heavier, like dolls' hair – squeaky.

A shade too big (or standing off respectfully)
it shrank your scalp; your face and eyes, too quick,
seemed dislocated, swerving like caught prey.

It gave you, not the judge's gravitas you needed
or the panto dame's bravado, but the frailty
of someone carrying a dead weight.

Out there was comedy: Crown Toppers,
ferrets, Ernie Wise. We banished quips
until you made them – made us smile

as you, who'd never cared about appearance
but half each year had worn Dad's socks around the house
took off the wig, turned it to the light

and felt the cavity inside:
the dull, flesh-coloured backing
where your warmth had been.

Escapology

I cannot ask about it now and you
would not have wanted to remember:
this little shot of you, Dad, nearly ten,
your sister just turned six, Auntie and someone
not your mother, backs to the chalet wall,
one chilly side of summer on the Wirral
frozen between happy and unhappy.

I cannot ask you now and when I could
you would have looked away, eyes stung
with remembered sand perhaps or shifting
as your pained bones recalled those picnic chairs
nowhere was level enough for, and how already
you were tired of being the older – oldest – child,
always being asked to know or do something.

I cannot ask about it now, and then
you would have cut loose: whisked us
via some show you might have seen around then
in New Brighton or just read about – some illusionist
you could demystify – from Wallasey to Singapore
and army days – the first and only place
(we didn't need to ask this) where you had felt safe.

In any case I know now how, when asked
to smile, you must have wondered in that instant
whether 'poorly' could mean going to die
(for some time now no one had said
your mother will pull through); I recognise
that sense, unnameable, of things going wrong,
that feeling of how hard it is to get life right

that froze your smile into a look of puzzlement
you bore until your last day and beyond.
Turning down *Songs of Praise* to hear you breathe,
the air thick with questions like a mass of wings
we felt it too as we sat helpless, knowing
how finally you were about to change the subject.

Afterwards

the house, for sale,
haemorrhages 'personal effects'.

Space replaces ornaments;
where pictures were, pale wallpaper
frames brighter memories.

Uneven stacks of books appear at windows,
their spines fading as behind them
rubber plants brown, fatally.

One afternoon a white van stands an hour or so
arms open like a priest's receiving all-comers:
small furniture, big boxes – carefully laid at first
till one bursts and shoes run down the drive
then shoved in any how; bin liners, bags
of odds and ends, long things down sides
a double eiderdown on top
the doors jammed shut.

A blue Metro perseveres, at weekends:
tools, computer stuff, bedside lamps, medication, pillows.
A quilt still in its cover. Box files.
Wads of unnamed photos.

Outside, the garden blurs.
The once-prim privet, undone, tries on lace.
Trees whisper. Dandelion clocks bide time.

The grass, empowered, climbs the steps
and waves.

Twentieth century

This is my aunt, my great-aunt Nellie Brown
(who lived, for what it was worth, to 101)
before her given name became a joke
standing at fifteen in the sea at Rhyl
some 20 feet from her younger sister's
photographic paraphernalia.

Her mother beside her looks unsure
but Nellie stands at ease – with life, with the breeze,
with the unfamiliar feel of her calves exposed to the sun
and the tickling surf: she looks us in the eye,
flexes her toes in the sand and sees who knows what
beyond the camera before her.

My aunt, before the twentieth century was born
when Rhyl was a day's jaunt in the charabanc
before the omnibus or motor car; before she saw
her grandmother burn in her nightdress by the hearth;
before they built the red brick market hall
at which the whole town kissed its youth goodbye.

My aunt, before she joined the VAD
before Edouard's last postcard from the front
before her brother came back maimed and silent;
before her sister's tumour let her claim
her niece and nephew and – in vain – their father;
before she nursed her parents to their slow deaths.

Before she took in the evacuees who would not eat,
before her brother turned to drink
and fathered a child she would not speak of,
before she kept house forty years for him
before she took in two stray cats for company
before the waiting rooms, the waiting lists…

before the home help helped herself
before the Queen misspelled her name
before the day-and-nightly moaning
from the next bed in the nursing home…

Before all this, before the breaking waves
my aunt stands, clutching her sepia petticoats knee-high
seeing a life that ripples and sparkles before her
and she smiles.

Over, near Winsford

Banked against the wall they lie, the flowers
grainy greys and whites. Beside a stretch of dark earth
under darker hessian, a sexton bends
to clear drifting cellophane. It's 1964 – the year
before our lives began in colour.

A corner plot must have meant status
for this Flanders amputee, who in my memory
is just a folded sleeve, a rag rug by an empty hearth
and once, a walk through wet fields
to admire some watercress.

I could track down the few feet
of that Cheshire grave, to read and almost own
the headstone telling me I stand above
a quarter of my blood. I check the faint note
on the photograph. A place called Over.

Learning to kiss

Full English

August was always Llandudno. Great Orme/Little Orme, Happy Valley,
someone on telly at the pier end. Half board at the pale green *Brig-y-Don*,
not too posh but central, opposite the bandstand. 8pm Wednesday concerts,
them black-jacketed, us watching from the bay, like royalty. Welsh words.
Who could say *Llanfairpwllgwyn* all the way to *gogogoch*.
How we forgot from year to year
what *Brig-y-Don* meant.

Mornings down in the basement, tots of 'proper' orange juice to savour
like communion wine before small bowls of cornflakes, then the platefuls
brought by smudge-eyed girls in nylons, skirts and thin school blouses.
How they'd been heard up late last night comparing parents, boyfriends.
How they did the butter curls. *Don't talk with your mouth full.*
High tide, how we felt cheated
by that stony strand.

No one forgets

Miss Phillipson, Miss Phillipson, why
did you smell and look so musty?
Did you sleep in a cupboard and wash in a pond
each day before you taught us?
No Dickens or Brontë could have dredged you up,
no crack designer have concocted
your brown crimplene suits
and yes it's a cliché but your tights *did* scratch
as you marched between the desks, barking
as we heard it 'where the bee sucks there suck I'

and yes, Miss Phillipson, you did
suck, we all thought, especially
the girls who learned from you they had
the wrong names or faces.

For my sins I let you sign my hymn book,
acknowledging the fact
that you were getting out before us –
off down south, of course –
but what was your parting shot?
Your exhortation for a girl to
make the most of what she'd got?
(Later I threw the book and
your *bons mots* into the Rochdale Canal):
'be good sweet maid
and let who will be clever' ?

Thanks, pal. Good teaching.
Right on, sister.
Thanks, Miss Phillipson.

Learning to kiss

Comings and goings are the danger zones:
hello, goodbye, goodnight and
how about a kiss?

Lesson one, the HORRIBLE after a clumsy hug:
some half-relative spatters you with licksmells,
lipstick, moist moustaches, whiffs of adulthood.
You learn to wash.

Lesson two, the TOLERABLE peck on the cheek:
an uncle or aunt stands still and makes you do the lot:
you learn to purse your lips and put them on course
for a dry bit of face.

Lesson three, the DESIRABLE, you teach yourself.
You glance through thickening living room air
at two-second clinches on films, study *Jackie* under desks
then dive in, sink or swim.

Lesson four, the SOCIAL. Unlearn all this and aim
for a not unpleasant collision of arms ears nose eyes lips.
I quite like you, you want to say. But don't.

Framed

That picture, Jan Van Eyck

Her gown is green,
the kind of green not often seen
indoors and much less
on a wedding dress:
the kind of green that startles
on an April morning after rain,
the green of fields in sudden sun,
of budding hawthorn leaves, of birth,
of growth, the green of
teeming, green of health –
and come to that
the green of wealth.

His gown is brown, or puce
as are his eyes –
the purple-brown of peat
through thinning heather,
the brown of careful husbandry,
the brown of money, study, heirlooms –
and of the darkest corners of the room
they're painted into.

Her skin is cream,
the cream of statuary,
the cream of parchment
yet to be inscribed,
the cream of luxury,
the cream of dreams.

The bed is red,
the red of embers,
the furnishings the red of blood
and their hearts –
as her eyes, pupil-black,
look past his left hand

neither claiming nor relinquishing
her own, not offered nor withheld
and past his right,
neither inviting nor denying
guests their time,
their centuries –
their hearts are colours
we can only guess.

Marginalia
i.m. MW

Suddenly hearing that you'd died,
meeting your grey eyes from that small obituary
caught me off guard, reeling in memories
of how tired you'd always looked –
more venerable, even then, than 28 years
could properly explain to me at seventeen.
Your early adulthood behind you, mine to come,
we occupied the margins of each other's minds, my fascination
just occasionally facing your bemusement head on
as I watched – and then began to help – you make your name,
writing it large on posters pieced together on bedsitter floors –
crude, but apparently inspired.

I have them still, flattened in some folder –
that and one or two lines pressed to the back of my mind.
Where can we go to make love in the city you threw out
mid-stanza to a standing audience.

If you can lose what you've not had, we lost touch
and head down in the swill of life I missed your star ascending,
your name larger on posters (professional this time but no more inspired),
your prizes – and that of all the venues waiting
there should have been
less than a mile between us for so long.

So that, meeting your gaze finally from that small obituary hooked me
from oblivion to wonder
where in the city I could go to mourn.

Apt pupil

Her father wanted her to be
a conjurer: to prestidigitate –
make things from nothing.

Fame, money, rabbits out of hats,
that kind of thing – exactly as
he would have done himself
if not for wars, work
and one thing or another

(and in small ways, later, did,
fixing together odds and ends
to give ailing household friends
a makeshift afterlife.

Something for nothing
except sweat and tears
his maxim).

And she would have learned
and been an apt pupil, if
her mother hadn't taught her first
to be invisible.

Nice work

In here I'm trying to write a poem
while out there a man has come
to clean the hall and landing carpet.
Paul Armitage's Home Cleaning Service,
van in drive, is feeding two diameters of hose
in through the windows, one sucks
while the other blows apparently
and *is it OK if I run the hot tap?*

In here I'm trying to write a poem
going back in time two thousand years.
Out there he *no I'm fine love, no,*
no problem starts up the compressor.
In here I'm hewing granite, out there
he squirts detergent on each stair in here
I'm hauling monoliths uphill on logs
out there he *may have to move the piano*
slightly

In here I'm chanting pagan funeral rites
out there I notice two different tones of suck
then intermittent thuds, clicks and bumps
advancing on the door which I get up and close,
properly, wondering how long
the quarrying took. Out there he's *going*
to have to try the bathroom window
in here I – oh, sod it.

Dusty answer

Lady, let's get this straight. That night you crashed up here
you woke the neighbours, shattering the silence like a diva.
Then you left early, when small morning courtesies
would have cost no more than the gin you finished
readily enough. You snored, too, as I recall: I turned my back,
glad of patterned wallpaper. You think I didn't sense you
prowling round, bumping into things as if to say you needed
space, more space. This is London. What did you expect
up all these stairs – a ranch? I heard you sniff, felt you
purse your lips and rip at everything with those incisor eyes.

Well let me tell you, when you're old that's what life is:
clutter. An unsightly mess of blessings, burdens and ephemera.
Pots break, windows get stuck down. You may flaunt
the scanty ingenuities of youth – white walls, straw mats,
babies and balloons. In winter, this place freezes.
'Tenant mice' must shift to take the edge off, keep warm,
stay the course. Red cushions are a comfort – a flat-warming gift;
your art's in words, mine in cherishing such kindnesses.
What's more, without a family, I have to be my own child
and mother – afford myself the love yours no doubt give you.

If you had striven for cosiness alone and got through decades
single-handed, you would not, I think, court emptiness.
No, I did not remove the roses before their malady offended –
you who were telling me you had sought out cadavers.
I don't deliberately keep wilting blooms, but as it happens
I can live with them: there is a certain lesson in their grace.
While you won scholarships in so-called taste, I learned
to take what comes and make the best of it. You have your prizes,
leave me mine. Given youth again I might choose differently

but could do worse. Some people there's no pleasing;
I fill the room with life: if you see death, that's your affair.
As I see it, you came, lapped up my hospitality and left
not empty-handed, but appropriating most of what I owned
to make a poem you wasted no time airing. I suppose
I should have known: you artists are all at it – thieving
for a living. Miss Bishop, mind you, was a little better mannered.
At least, she seemed to find the dust amusing.

Thank you for thinking of us

no shards, no lozenges, no litanies
no seagulls, no patinas
no abstract nouns, no adjectives or very few
no haiku

no feelings named, no jokes explained
no smart-arse quips, no rock lyrics
no cats, no dogma

no chopping herbs at kitchen windowsills
no shock tactics, no eating afterbirth
no highbrow quotes, no dream tropes

no obscure myths
no bits in foreign languages
no Shakespeare for the sake of it
no lists like this
no ellipses like these...

no one-word lines, no full rhymes
(unless you're Tony Harrison)
no sing-song rhythms – no *di-dum*
di-dum di-dum, di-dum di-dum

no facile puns, no lies, no libel, no obscenities
no soul-baring
no lambent, incandescent anything
no slips in tone or register

and hey –
no publisher

Jump!

I am a child planted on a path which curves away.
Ahead, my parents, who just minutes ago held my hand
have let go, walked off and are leaving me.

I watch. They don't look back and I don't say –
don't want to know there's nothing I can do
to turn them round.

I'm on my own now, falling back through years
onto a kindly held-out blanket – who holds that? –
of memories from which I bounce back up, up

onto my father's or my mother's shoulders, light enough
to ride there like an empress with the wide world at my feet
mine for the asking and the sun an outstretched hand away.

But I grow – I grow too big and heavy for them,
weigh their strong young adult bodies down
as they must have their parents, groundwards.

Swaying, I look back down a tower of acrobats:
strong men and women who as their feet sank deeper into clay
reached skywards with their children.

But I have none: no child to lift onto my shoulders
(or walk away from). Yet as their concentrated sinews
urge in me some *tour de force*

I look round for some high point I can jump to –
feel their voices rising through me – *Jump*, they're saying
and I'm saying *jump*, now –

Thank you

for the long weekend.
It was a long one, wasn't it?
Thank you for clearing off your friends
and tidying your room so much I thought I'd strayed next door;
for placing that brand new box of tissues by your single bed,
changing the sheets, plumping the pillow
                                    and somehow getting the quilt so smooth
it looked as if you'd ironed it *in situ*;
                    for combing (though not, apparently, washing) your hair
then sitting there peeling an orange over Marvell thinking I'd take you for one.
And thank you for later coming, as you put it, clean –
saying you'd always hoped my no meant yes
and tossing a rancid sleeping bag onto the adjacent junk room floor.

Thank you, but
you really shouldn't have.

Valentine

It was you, wasn't it?
Sent me a box of genitalia?
Not two but twenty-four ripe ovaries
with six enormous stamens each engorged with pollen
thrusting purple-veined through curvy lips and downy inner folds
around a fleshy pistil glistening with a film of moisture round the swollen tip
all bursting from a flushed, moist, hirsute declivity and smelling...
as if freshly showered?

Thank you for the flowers.
I won't read too much into it.

Pausing on SEND

New Year's Eve. Looking for beer, you find me
by the back door, downing tears. We slip like fallen angels
up the path between the throbbing house and crusty garage.
I'm sober and it must be freezing but I hardly care.

Not quite strangers but far from close, you take my arm
like someone out of Jane Austen leading in to dinner
up the narrow cul-de-sac. Your words calm,
I snuffle, gasping, through snagged breath.

Till now we've almost never not talked shop.
You stop to comfort me and as we move on, gently
leave your arm there. Past front gardens, weeping willows,
semis past their bedtime, other couples seeing us as one,

up past the park across from rows of pretty terraces
where proper people live, people who know,
who've found out somehow, how. Your arm still there
past sheltered housing, wheelie bins in pairs,

we're steps away now from the main road, taxis,
tough oblivion. These city arteries all strange to me,
unreal in sodium, your arm still there, I feel how near I am
to being lost. I do not even know what year it is.

I hear you're happy now, as you deserve to be, married
with kids, career. This is to thank you, twenty, twenty-one
years on. To tell you that I feel your arm still there
light as a wing, as words, gathering.

Waltz

Married fifty years today, Ted and Edie
take the floor not needing onlookers, but pleased
for those who want to watch their Anniversary Waltz.
They bring their language from another world
of sweethearts, long engagements and apprenticeships
in which they practised drawing and respecting
boundaries, making choices at every turn
yet making believe there was no other way.
If asked, they'd say theirs was no mystery, just years
of graft, of grasping drifts and judging distances,
steering a course through fractured families, neighbours,
nations – weaving meaning into remnant spaces –
station platforms, backyards, beaches – patterning
the long and short sides of their years until they learned
to keep in step, beating time, being alive together.
Now warmed by applause they cross the boards
and, holding and yet not quite being held,
teach us the grace of gentle intimacy. They wear
the clothes they walked here in, but in the light confetti
of the mirrorball the years fall from them
and they twirl their wedding finery, still points
at the centre of a dancing world.

Without a dog

Viking funeral
after Sir Frank Bernard Dicksee

To live and die by fire and the sword,
the loss spectacular, the pyre heaped with spoils moving
as if still impelled by life towards a livid sky,
the sea embracing what the flames must leave, this rite
had dignity: an end more worth the fight than some
slow pacing of the grey land down to musty dark.
Seeing the craft shrink to a wave-rocked cradle
you might think its passenger a child again,
finding the years of sleep life stole from them.
Eyes stung by wind, voices torn by shingle,
each bay-dweller bore this image far beyond that dawn
in verse and song across the waves from *vik* to *vaig*
to *wick* to *way* to *bay*, to be cast up on nameless shores
as orphan fragments, pasts spun from their opacity
like light still shining from a dead star.

vik *(Icelandic) n. bay, has these and other North European variants*

Plenty

We have plenty of pens in our house, the ones sent by charities
that prod you like a bone in the envelope and your heart sinks
because you really wanted a letter from a friend. Instead

the bone in the envelope comes with a headline saying
IN THE TIME IT TAKES YOU TO READ THIS
ANOTHER CHILD WILL DIE. And you feel guilty

because it's always a white pen containing just enough blue ink
to sign your name and start a small shopping list but
white is the colour for paper not pens, which should be black,

so you stick it with all the rest in the shepherd and shepherdess
spill holders that came from your gran's and look as if
they might be valuable if they weren't full of pens

and get on with the rest of your day, wording replies
in the back of your mind like *I do not respond to emotional blackmail.*
And next day in the post you get a pair of smiley slippers.

To be or not to be

To give a little bit to every cause that sends a begging letter
or just some? Which ones then and how much?
Or put cash in collection boxes and risk looking smug
or just keep clearing cupboards and donating junk?
But is that really a donation if it's stuff that you don't want?

To hang the washing out with those clouds over there
and have to keep an eye on it or stick it in the dryer
and return those library books? But could that be dangerous?
I mean you hear of people coming home to find the house on fire
and even if it wasn't would the shirts all be too creased?
REDUCED IRON. What is that supposed to mean?

To tax the car for six months or a year or sell the thing
before it rusts to bits and we get stung for hundreds more
to get it through its MOT – and go by bus and just be done with it?
But if it didn't come and I was late for work?
Not that I'd need the extra money probably without the car
but aren't there other reasons why I work? And drive?

To book a decent holiday or stay here, save ourselves the stress
and creosote the shed before it falls apart – and weed the lawn?
Dig out the biggest dandelions and watch them all come back
or blitz the lot with *Weed n' Feed* and have to put up
with those brown patches instead? Scorched earth, that is – as bad as Vietnam.
But not on the same scale. Or is it, when you add up all the lawns?

To face the fact that I'm not getting any younger, give up colouring my hair
(the scalp absorbs those chemicals, I read somewhere) and let it all go grey?
How long would that take and who would be most affected, me or others?
How much money would I save? Can't work it out. Because the chemicals
have killed too many brain cells already? Or was that all the beer in my 20s?

To cook a proper meal tonight or have baked beans and does that go with
wine?
Then red or white?

To watch the news and let it get to me or be a philistine, go straight to bed and get an early night?

Tea or coffee?

Cup or Gary Larson mug?

That is the question.

Without a dog

I did the walk we did at New Year, backwards –
stopped the tapes of *Crimewatch* in my head.
This day is mine, I said, *I'll have it.*
On your own? I wavered, on the stile.
The field's exposed, you could be watched.
That hollow by the stream could hide – . *No.*
I claimed this February Friday's eggblue sky
and cloud-wrapped green as mine –
a birthday right. I did not need a lead.

I jumped defiant into deep wet grass
as if I owned the scene, its colours vivid
as a children's book. *Look,* I challenged watchers,
look! An out-of-season ladybird on granite
like a drop of blood. A catkin, hanging
from a bare tree like a pilot light.
I strode across the brook and up the meadow
to the kissing gate, the woods I trusted
surely no more sinister today than they had been
for centuries without me. Hearing voices
deep ahead I did not quicken or change tack.
Just men, I thought, just talking.
                              Quiet,
except for twigs and flitting birds, I paused
in stillness. Then I crossed the thickest dark
to come out at the broken fence
and up the old church lane – deserted.
High above, a woodpecker flew out
across a vaulted openness. For me, for me.
Unbelieving, yet obscurely needing
to give thanks, I nodded back to God's house
as I walked, dogless, safely home to mine.

Faith in our times

I *Desiderata*

Let me win the lottery.
Let my indolence be deeply satisfying,
my new-found friends exude integrity,
my chauffeur drive me soberly,
my white stretch limousine be
inconspicuous, low-key.

Let my investments
be low-risk, high-growth,
my helicopter safe as houses.
Let my media be favourable,
my paparazzi self-effacing,
my *Sun* reporters even-handed, fair.

Let my gluttony be flattering,
my lusts acceptable,
my drugs designer-pure,
my year-round tan not ageing nor
malignant. Let my plastic surgeon have
the hand of Michelangelo.

Let my paradise be well protected,
my gates electrified,
my stalkers all pre-empted.
Let the gun beside my bed be loaded,
my aim be true
and let my sleep be dreamless.

II *Cold call*

In the end you know they'll come for you
though you won't see them darkening the door:
Gothic, improbable throwbacks from some body's past
out of place but chillingly at home,
their white shirts luminous against
their strangely worn dark suits,
their flesh plausible enough but their expressions
ill-composed. Three of them. One fingers a hat
lifted from some bleak melodrama. Two hang back:
one with a holdall, heavy, black. Don't ask.

After formalities they'll leave them to it, your protectors
opening and closing doors like rank conspirators –
and after so long fighting you won't lift a finger either
but let them – stitch you up, truss you, robe you
outlandishly as they see fit, until
you are no longer you but some cold clone
that submits to be carried, silent, prone,
out from your earthly home
towards some other   alien   unknown.

Lost

We call them lost, our loved ones, but if they are
just that – lost – wandering among the stars, faint
as our faith in heaven or hell, knowing other fates –

like that recurring dream of being lost in an echo
of a place where nothing's recognised and no one
recognises you, of wandering without a haven,
without welcome, without knowing where you are
except that you were, once, on earth but where is that,
oh mother, father, child, if you are more lost there
than you were here, what then?   What then?